As Aesop Complained To The Brothers Grimmly

# you turned the fables on me

Written and Illustrated By Barry Geller

**PRICE/STERN/SLOAN**
*Publishers, Inc., Los Angeles*

Copyright © 1978 By Barry Geller
Published by Price/Stern/Sloan Publishers, Inc.
410 North La Cienega Boulevard
Los Angeles, California 90048
Printed in the United States of America
All rights reserved.
ISBN #0-8431-0477-5

# HANS HANDERSON
# And His Sons
# Hans

Once there was
a man named Hans.

Hans  and his
beau tiful wife,

Gretchen  and

their **11** handsome

sons

lived in a large, modern, split-

level,

all electric
model home...

in a comfortable
community called
Celestial Gardens,

...near a seaside suburb of the centrally located, culturally conscious, contemporary city of Centerville.

**Hans was a
master electrician,
but, alas, he was
completely incapable**

**of any sort of
creative thinking**

This explains why
all 11 sons were
also named Hans.

What could poor
Gretchen say? If
she complained, Hans
would get cranky and
pull the fuses and
then the lights would

...go out...

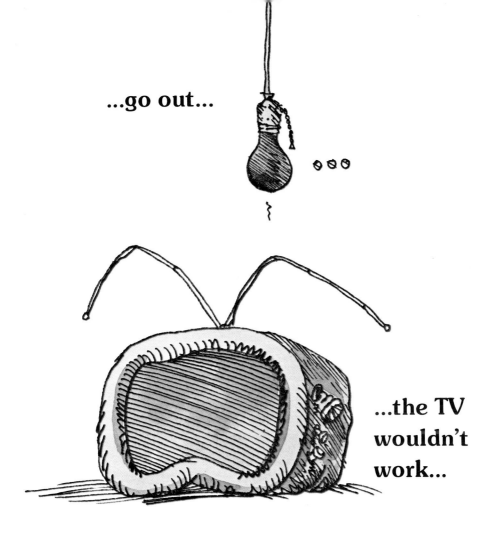

...the TV
wouldn't
work...

and the freezer
would
defrost.

**One day this
was exactly what
happened.**

**And in the flick of a
switch they all came.**

**They all hurried to
their assignments
and in a short time...**

...everything was on.

Each one claimed the
credit, but they
never really knew who
fixed the lights.

**But we know...
don't we?**

There is a very
old and very wise
saying that goes
like this...

*"Many Hans*
*make light work."*

# THE GOLDEN HEART

This is Farrah Maiden.
She has beautiful golden hair
with full body, natural waves,
sweet smells, no split ends,
and no frizzies.

She loves a king.
He is a grouch.

**This is King Crabby**
**He has itchy scalp, watery eyes,**
**gray teeth, bad breath, a wrinkled vest,**
**dirty finger nails, baggy britches**
**and holes in his socks.**

**He never smiles.**

**But Farrah Maiden loves him
just the same.**

Everytime he passes by she smiles
and he frowns —
or doesn't even notice her at all.

One day she could no longer bear
the silence. She decided to speak.
She had to tell him of her love.

As he passed by she said,
"Sire, I am only Farrah Maiden with
golden hair and I have nothing to offer
you but my love and my heart.
If you will but speak to me,
I will give you my heart."

"What good will your love do me?"
grumped the king,
"Will it pay my soldiers?

And as for your heart,
it would only be useful to me
if it were as gold as your hair."


Well, with that,
Farrah Maiden began to cry.

She cried, and cried, and cried,
until she began to dissolve.

With her last sob
she was completely gone,
melted away.
All that remained on the floor
at King Crabby's feet was her heart —
as golden as her hair had been —
in the middle of
a big puddle of water.

The King bent down
and picked up the heart,
dried it off on his robe,
scratched it to see if it was
solid gold, and called a servant
to dry the floor.

"I hope it doesn't leave a stain on the hardwood," he complained as he sloshed away in his soggy socks.

The moral?

*"Never put the heart before the coarse."*

# NO LEAN DIET

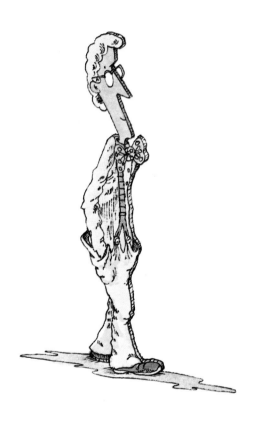

**Jack Spratt could eat no fat,**

**his wife could eat no lean . . .**

**That is until one day when
she looked at herself in a mirror.**

"I'm getting a bit pudgy," she burped
as she tried to tie her apron around
her waist. Right then and there,
she decided to go on a diet.

She didn't go on just one diet,
she tried every diet known
to man or beast.

She ate high protein,
she ate low calorie,
she ate only fruit,
only vegetables,
she ate mucousless,
she ate saltless,
she ate waterless,
she ate cottage cheese,
she ate sea weed,
she ate herbs,
she ate legumes,
she ate alfalfa sprouts,
she ate appetite depressant pills,
she ate crackers that
swell up in your stomach,
she ate seeds,
she ate nuts,
she ate yogurt.

She even saw a doctor who
did acupuncture.
He put a wire in her ear lobe
which was supposed to make
her lose her appetite.
He called it his "staple diet."
It didn't work.

Nothing worked!

She just kept getting bigger
and bigger.
Finally she said to Jack,
"I've tasted every diet known
to man or beast.
Why do I keep getting
bigger and bigger?"

**Jack stood and thought for a few moments and then said lovingly,**

*"Taste makes waist."*

# MAZDA

"Hi!, I'm the light's witch.
I go by the name of Mazda.

I live in lightenment.
I work nights, and have my days off.
It's kind of a 'burn out job.'

You know what really turns me on?
Knowledge!

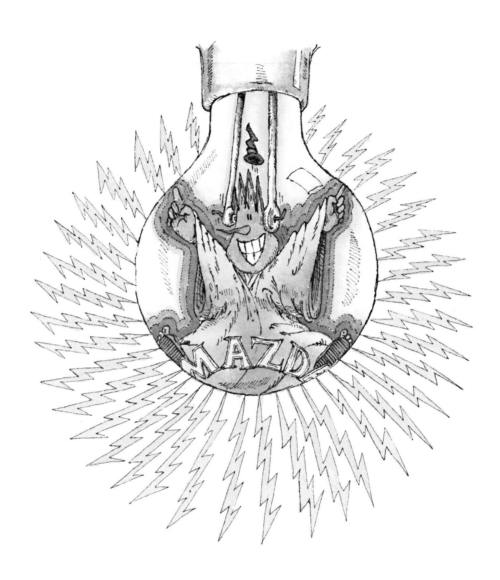

I'll shed some light on that subject.
Knowledge is only real
when you have experience with it.
That's true knowledge . . .
not just current events.

That's why I go out every day,
for experience.

**I don't just live in a vacuum.
I've been around the globe
thousands of times.**

I don't mean to boast,
but no light in the world
can shine without me.

So pay attention to watt I say
and don't just take it lightly.
Ignorance is darkness;
it turns you off.
Knowledge is light.

That's my message to you,
it's my 'mazdapiece.'"

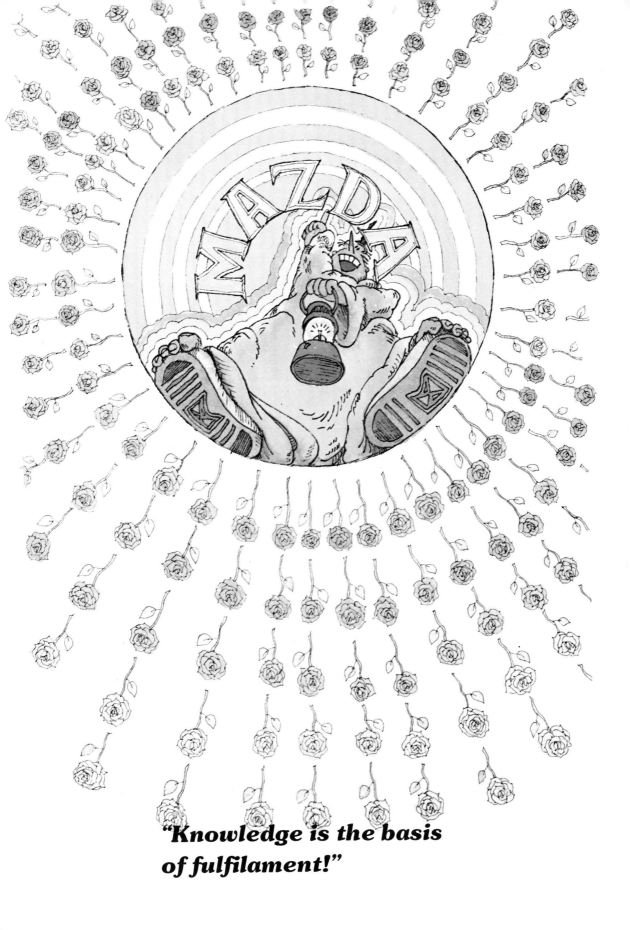

*"Knowledge is the basis
of fulfilament!"*

# LOUIE THE LAP

I love laps.

**A lap is a gap above the knees
and below the solar plexis.**

It's an 'L made by a lady or a
gentleman when they settle in a sofa,
or sittle in a chair.

**That's when a lap is there.**

Laps are warm and cozy,
luxurious and lovable,
soft and comfortable,
safe and secure,

**and magic.**

I can not figure out where laps go
when people stand up.

**I will do anything
to be able to lie in a lap.
Any time,
any place,
any where at all.**

**I will even do tricks.**

I will beg,

speak,

**sit,**

stay,

roll over,

fetch,

count,

**heel,**

**or play dead.**

**I'll even take a bath
to sit in a lap.**

Let's face it, I'm a lap dog.
I'm lap happy.

One day, just after lunch,
Larry's sister Louise was making
a lap in the living room.

She was listening to a cello concert
by Pablo Casals and really loving it,
or maybe she was falling asleep.

Anyhow, I was lying in the hall
by the front door when I first
noticed the appearance of the lap.

**I didn't wait for an invitation
-- or even take a second look.**

I scrambled to my paws,
slipped on the vinyl tiles,
peeled out, ran across the rug

**and leapt into the air with
the intention of a lappy landing.**

**Oh, unlucky leap!**

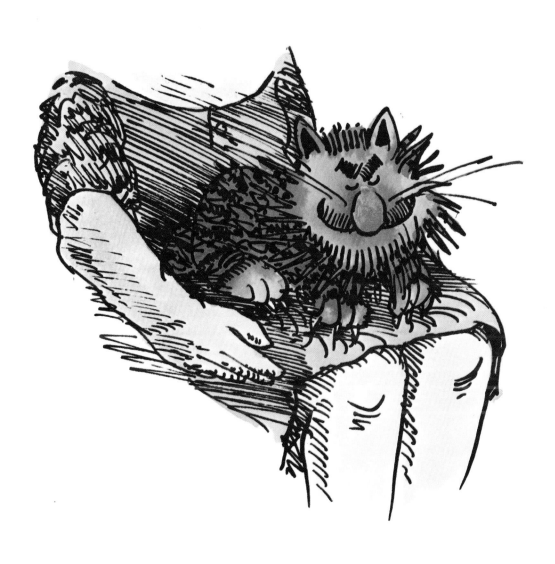

**Louise's lap was full of
sleeping Lucifer, unwelcome feline
lying in lapland,
right where I was landing.**

Well, you can imagine the rest.

I learned my lesson.

*"Always look before you lap."*

**P.S. Everything turned out O.K.**

A little later Lucifer went out
for his evening jog around the block.
Louise turned on television to watch
Lassie and made her lap again.
This time I waited for an invitation,
and settled comfortably
in the lap of luxury.

*"He who laps last, laps best."*

**PRICE/STERN/SLOAN**
*Publishers, Inc., Los Angeles*